W0114682

This journal belongs to

....

Date

....

Hope is the anchor of our souls. I know of no one who is not in need of hope—young or old, strong or weak, rich or poor.

JAMES E. FAUST

Live well, live wisely, live humbly. It's the way you live,
not the way you talk, that counts.

THE BIBLE

We should not moor a ship with one anchor, or our life with one hope.

EPICTETUS

Strength does not come from winning. Your struggles develop your strengths.
When you go through hardships and decide not to surrender, that is strength.

ARNOLD SCHWARZENEGGER

Without moral and intellectual independence,
there is no anchor for national independence.

DAVID BEN-GURION

Everyone has a gift for something, even if it is the gift of being a good friend.

MARIAN ANDERSON

My faith is what serves as the anchor and directs my actions.

JOHN THUNE

When you go through deep waters, I will be with you.
When you go through rivers of difficulty, you will not drown.

THE BIBLE

Bad things happen. If you're not anchored, you're going to be washed away.

DABO SWINNEY

Becoming successful in anything requires perseverance.

NICHOLAS SPARKS

Strength lies in differences, not in similarities.

STEPHEN COVEY

A hero is an ordinary individual who finds the strength to persevere
and endure in spite of overwhelming obstacles.

CHRISTOPHER REEVE

Perhaps I am stronger than I think.

THOMAS MERTON

I am not afraid of storms, for I am learning how to sail my ship.

LOUISA MAY ALCOTT

Do you have an anchor? I have found that a solid anchor
is indispensable to one who intends to live life fully.
To have an anchor is to be centered and well grounded.

STEVE GOODIER

God's grace is strong enough to hold me steady through every difficulty.

LAILAH GIFTY AKITA

Go boldly and honestly through the world.
Learn to love the fact that there is nobody else quite like you.

DANIEL RADCLIFFE

Have an anchor so that life doesn't toss you around.

DEBBY RYAN

Listen to what you know instead of what you fear.

RICHARD BACH

I think scars are like battle wounds—beautiful, in a way. They show what you've been through and how strong you are for coming out of it.

God alone is my rock and my salvation, my fortress where I will not be shaken.

THE BIBLE

You can do anything you set your mind to, but it takes
action, perseverance, and facing your fears.

GILLIAN ANDERSON

Be like the cliff against which the waves continually break;
but it stands firm and tames the fury of the water around it.

MARCUS AURELIUS

Don't expect to build up the weak by pulling down the strong.

CALVIN COOLIDGE

Storms make the oak grow deeper roots.

GEORGE HERBERT

The undertaking of a new action brings new strength.

RICHARD L. EVANS

Today is unique! It has never occurred before, and it will never be repeated. At midnight it will end, quietly, suddenly, totally. Forever. But the hours between now and then are opportunities with eternal possibilities.

CHARLES R. SWINDOLL

The battle is not to the strong alone; it is to the vigilant, the active, the brave.

PATRICK HENRY

There is meaning in every journey that is unknown to the traveler.

DIETRICH BONHOEFFER

Cast your cares on God; that anchor holds.

FRANK MOORE COLBY

If you can't fly, then run; if you can't run, then walk; if you can't walk, then crawl; but whatever you do, you have to keep moving forward.

MARTIN LUTHER KING JR.

Hope is the anchor of life.

LAILAH GIFTY AKITA

Put your feet in the right place, then stand firm.

ABRAHAM LINCOLN

I am somebody…I am me. I like being me,
and I need nobody to make me a somebody.

LOUIS L'AMOUR

Obstacles are things a person sees when he takes his eyes off his goal.

E. JOSEPH COSSMAN

Life has no remote. Get up and change it yourself!

MARK A. COOPER

I arise today through a mighty strength: God's power to guide me.

BRIDGID OF GAEL

As we let our own light shine, we subconsciously give
other people permission to do the same.

MARIANNE WILLIAMSON

Courage does not always roar. Sometimes courage is the quiet voice
at the end of the day saying, "I will try again tomorrow."

MARY ANNE RADMACHER

He turns not back who is bound to a star.

LEONARDO DA VINCI

Copyright © 2019 by Ellie Claire

Cover by Melissa Reagan. Cover copyright © 2019 by Hachette Book Group, Inc.

Hachette Book Group supports the right to free expression and the value of copyright. The purpose of copyright is to encourage writers and artists to produce the creative works that enrich our culture.

The scanning, uploading, and distribution of this book without permission is a theft of intellectual property. If you would like permission to use material from the book (other than for review purposes), please contact permissions@hbgusa.com.

Ellie Claire
Hachette Book Group
1290 Avenue of the Americas, New York, NY 10104
ellieclaire.com

First edition: September 2019

Ellie Claire is a division of Hachette Book Group, Inc. The Ellie Claire name and logo are trademarks of Hachette Book Group, Inc.

The publisher is not responsible for websites (or their content) that are not owned by the publisher.

Scripture quotations are from: The Holy Bible, New Living Translation (NLT). Copyright © 1996, 2004, 2007 by Tyndale House Foundation. Used by permission of Tyndale House Publishers Inc., Carol Stream, Illinois 60188. | The Message (MSG). Copyright © 1993, 1994, 1995, 1996, 2000, 2001, 2002. Used by permission of NavPress Publishing Group.

Compiled by Rachel F. Overton.
Print book interior design by Bart Dawson.

ISBN: 9781546014386 (Leatherluxe®)

Printed in China
RRD-S
10 9 8 7 6 5 4 3 2 1

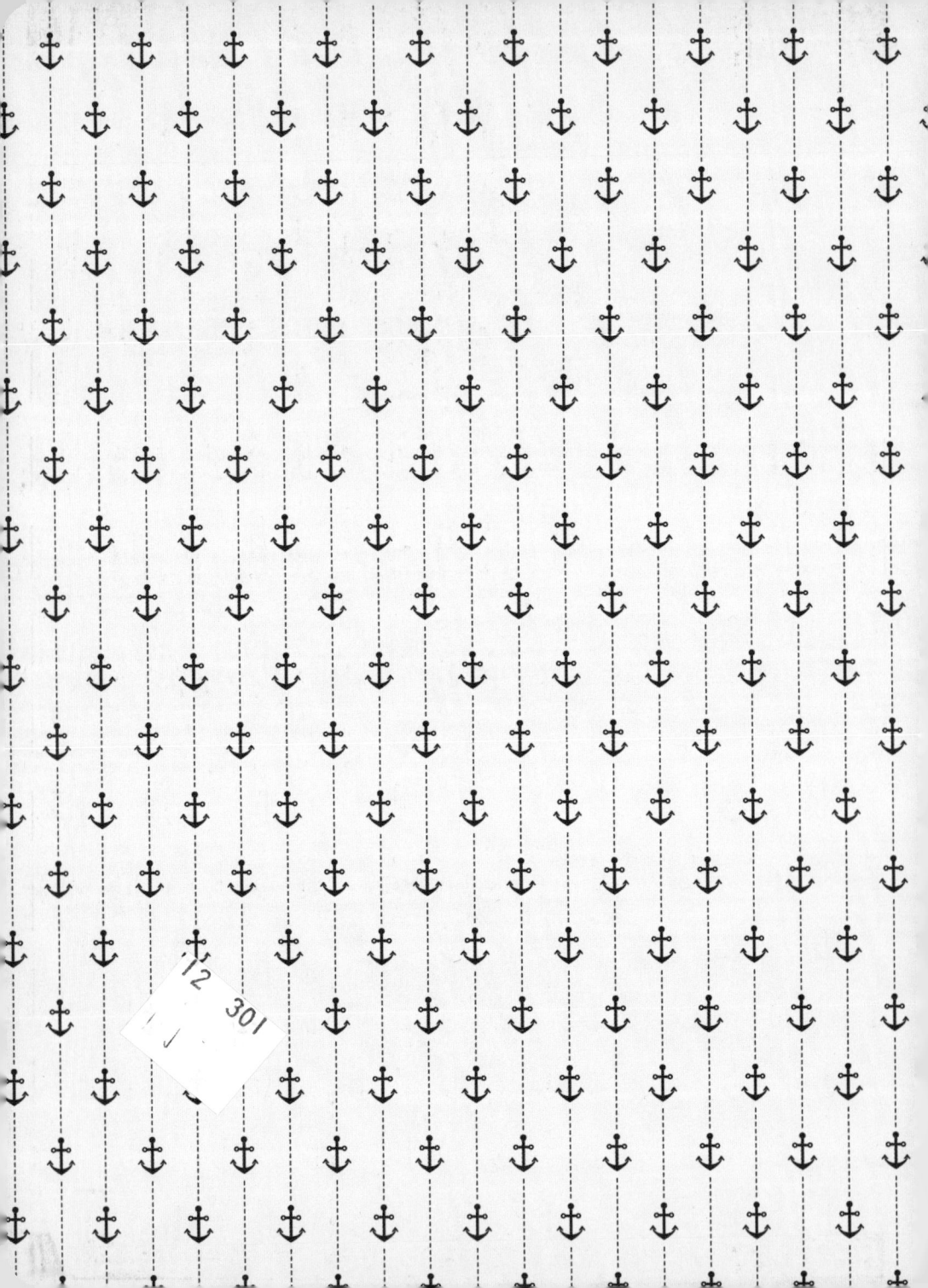